Celebrating
**Hispanic
Diversity**

THE PEOPLE
AND CULTURE OF
VENEZUELA

Elizabeth Borngraber

PowerKiDS
press.
New York

Published in 2018 by The Rosen Publishing Group, Inc.
29 East 21st Street, New York, NY 10010

First Edition

Editor: Theresa Morlock
Book Design: Rachel Rising

Photo Credits: Cover Inti St Clair/Blend Images/Getty Images; Cover (background) apomares/E+/Getty Images; Cover, p. 1 https://en.wikipedia.org/wiki/File:Flag_of_Venezuela_(state).svg; p. 5 iStockphoto.com/jimmyvillalta; p. 7 Alice Nerr/Shutterstock.com; p. 9 davidluna/RooM/Getty Images; p. 11 FEDERICO PARRA/Stringer/AFP/Getty Images; p. 12 Kobby Dagan/Shutterstock.com; p. 13 Horst P. Horst/ Conde Nast Collection/Getty Images; p. 15 JUAN BARRETO/AFP/Getty Images; p. 17 GUILLERMO LEGARIA/AFP/Getty Images; p. 19 https://commons.wikimedia.org/wiki/File:Yukpa_dance.jpg; p. 21 Raphael GAILLARDE/Gamma-Rapho/Getty Images p. 23 Everett Historical/Shutterstock.com; p. 24 Olaf Speier/Shutterstock.com; p. 25 EDUARDO SOTERAS/AFP/Getty Images; p. 27 Photo Works/Shutterstock.com; p. 29 Shaun Botterill/Getty Images Sport/Getty Images; p. 30 Brothers Good/Shutterstock.com.

Cataloging-in-Publication Data

Names: Borngraber, Elizabeth.
Title: The people and culture of Venezuela / Elizabeth Borngraber
Description: New York : PowerKids Press, 2018. | Series: Celebrating Hispanic diversity | Includes index.
Identifiers: ISBN 9781538327036 (pbk.) | ISBN 9781508163077 (library bound) | ISBN 9781538327470 (6 pack)
Subjects: LCSH: Venezuela–Juvenile literature. | Venezuela–Social life and customs–Juvenile literature.
Classification: LCC F2308.5 B67 2018 | DDC 987–dc23

Manufactured in the United States of America

CPSIA Compliance Information: Batch #BW18PK: For Further Information contact Rosen Publishing, New York, New York at 1-800-237-9932

CONTENTS

A DIVERSE LAND

The Bolivarian Republic of Venezuela is filled with many landscapes and natural resources that add to its beauty. The **culture** of Venezuela is the beautiful result of different cultures mixing together. After **colonization** began in the 1500s, Spanish, African, and **indigenous** cultures began to blend. Most people can trace their family back to a combination of these cultures.

As a country of **immigrants**, most Venezuelans are of mixed **heritage**. The word for people of mixed Spanish and indigenous heritage is mestizo. These combinations resulted in a rich mixture of cultural traditions. More than 31 million people live and work in Venezuela. All contribute to the ever-changing culture of their country while coming together under the united flag of Venezuela.

Language Is Important

You may have heard people use the term "Hispanic" to describe people when they actually meant to say "Latino." These terms are often confused, but they can't be used the same way. "Latino" is a term for a person living in the United States whose **ancestors** are from Latin America. Some people don't use either term to describe themselves. When someone tells you how to talk about their identity, it's important to respect that by using the language they prefer.

TIERRA DE GRACIA

On his third voyage to America, Christopher Columbus landed in Venezuela while exploring the Gulf of Paria in 1498. He was amazed by the area's beauty. He called it Tierra de Gracia, which means "Land of Grace." Venezuela is home to many exciting landscapes, including miles of coastlines, mountains, and forests.

Venezuela is located on the northern tip of South America. It has 1,740 miles (2,800 km) of coastline that touch the Caribbean Sea and the Atlantic Ocean. On the western side of the country, the Andes Mountains stretch toward the sea. Hills and valleys cover most of the southeast, with large *tepuis* bordering Brazil. *Tepuis* are mountains with flat tops. The *tepuis* have rainy and dry seasons, just like the rest of Venezuela.

At 3,212 feet (979 m) tall, Angel Falls in Venezuela is the tallest waterfall in the world. It was the inspiration for Paradise Falls in the 2009 Disney/Pixar movie *Up*.

Biodiversity

Venezuela features great biodiversity, which means the country is home to many plant and animal species, or kinds. Nearly 250 species of mammals live in Venezuela, including jaguars, sloths, pumas, and howler monkeys. Venezuela is also home to the anaconda, the largest snake in the world. Many plants and flowers are found in the Amazon region of the country and atop the towering *tepuis*.

NATIVE PEOPLES

Long ago, Venezuela was home to many indigenous peoples who made their homes in tropical jungles and along the coastline. The different landscapes of the country caused each group to develop its own **unique** culture, language, and way of living.

One group, the Chibchas, lived in the Andes Mountains as farmers. They grew vegetables such as maize (corn) and potatoes. Along the rivers, groups such as the **nomadic** Warao lived as hunters and gatherers. The Añu, a coastal group, built houses on wooden poles to protect themselves from snakes. Living near the water provided a steady source of food such as fish and other wildlife.

Some indigenous people still live in Venezuela today and make up a small part of the population. Most make their homes in the Amazon rain forest and other distant parts of the country.

Members of the Warao people and many other groups still live along the Orinoco River.

Slavery in Venezuela

In the late 1500s, Spanish explorers founded many new settlements in Venezuela. They were looking to make money through trade and by finding items such as pearls and gold. These new settlers fought wars with the indigenous groups of the region. Native people often lost these battles, and the Europeans made them into slaves. During this time, the Spanish also forced many African people to come to Venezuela as slaves.

RELIGIOUS BELIEFS

As more people arrived in Venezuela, the cultures of native groups mixed with Spanish, European, and African traditions to form new religious beliefs. Today, almost 90 percent of Venezuelans are Roman Catholic, while the rest are mostly Protestant, Jewish, or Muslim. Catholic Mass can be heard daily in local churches.

Many Venezuelans also worship María Lionza, a healer with fair skin and green eyes who was the daughter of a native chief. There are many **legends** about María Lionza, and a statue of her stands in Caracas, the capital of Venezuela. Her followers perform **rituals** to call down spirits who help with healing and seeing the future. These rituals involve music, dance, and offerings to spirits.

A follower of María Lionza walks through flames during a ritual.

CLOTHING STYLES

Native peoples normally dress in handmade fabrics, which they wrap around themselves. However, most Venezuelans wear Western-style clothing that is also right for the climate. Traditional Venezuelan clothing is usually worn only for special occasions.

The traditional Mexican dress worn by this woman is similar to the colorful dresses worn in Venezuela

This man is wearing a traditional *liqui-liqui* outfit.

The traditional outfit for men is called the *liqui-liqui*, which is a shirt and pants made of white cotton with gold buttons. They can also be fastened with leather or a sash. This outfit is similar to what the llanero, or traditional Venezuelan herdsmen, used to wear. Classic dress for women is ruffled blouses with long skirts. These skirts can come in any number of colors. For festivals, clothing can vary from traditional dress to elaborate and colorful costumes.

HOLIDAYS AND FESTIVALS

As a Roman Catholic country, many of Venezuela's holidays and festivals are connected to religious days. The most popular is Carnival, which is celebrated in the days before Ash Wednesday. A large parade marks the beginning of the celebration. People dress in fancy costumes and spend most of their time dancing and singing traditional songs.

Christmas has historically been a big celebration in Venezuela, with families setting up **nativity scenes** and singing in the evening. Venezuelans celebrate Christmas from mid-December until January 6. Traditionally, the Three Kings, not Santa Claus, bring gifts for children.

Other important festivals are held for patron saint days. Each Venezuelan village has its own patron saint, which is celebrated through dress and music. Each village has its own way of honoring its saint.

Costumed people gather in the street to dance and perform for Carnival.

15

BOLD SOUNDS

The national music of Venezuela is joropo. Joropo is a style of folk music and is part of a large group of styles called *música llanera*. Joropo may be performed with poetry and dancing. This musical style is traditionally played with a harp and maracas, though different regions of the country have other traditions. Other folk music styles include *gaita*, which is played at festivals and Christmastime.

The cuatro, a four-string guitar, is the national instrument of Venezuela. The country is also home to many different styles of harps, which are traditionally used in folk music. Venezuelan music today shows signs of Spanish, African, and native influences. The most popular styles are salsa, merengue, and reggaeton. Oscar D'Leon, a famous salsa musician who created 60 albums, is a Venezuelan native.

Music is a great source of pride for Venezuela. Both the Venezuelan Symphony Orchestra and the Simón Bolívar Youth Orchestra attract great musicians from around the country to perform.

EXCITING MOVES

Dance is as much an important part of Venezuelan culture as music. Indigenous people used dance to celebrate festivals and yearly feasts. These dances combined with those of early settlers to create the dances performed by Venezuelan artists today. Most modern Venezuelan festivals have some form of traditional music and dance featured in their celebrations.

Ballet in Venezuela involves traditional dance as well as more modern styles. Ballet International de Caracas performed the joropo dance across Latin America and the United States in the 1970s, while many companies now perform classical forms of ballet. Today, the most popular kinds of dance are salsa and *cumbia*, which is slower than salsa.

Yukpa people perform a traditional dance for a crowd in downtown Caracas.

19

COLORFUL MASTERPIECES

Venezuelan art has taken many forms over the years. Early people created necessary tools and items such as handmade instruments, pottery, blankets, and baskets. Natural materials, such as coconut husks, palm fibers, and wool, were used to create these colorful works. Many of today's indigenous people still create the same folk art as their ancestors.

Religious traditions inspired most sculptures and paintings in the 1800s, though this has changed in recent years. Many different styles influence modern artists, who often blend **abstract** elements into their work. Another style that has become popular is kinetic art, in which artists create pieces that move or look like they move. It's common to see modern Venezuelan works of art with bold colors and shapes.

Jesús Soto, pictured here, was a well-known kinetic artist from Venezuela.

Architecture

During colonial times, Spanish art styles helped shape Venezuelan architecture. Buildings were very simple, and brick and tiles were commonly used. After the country won its independence, abstract styles became more popular, and people destroyed or changed many old buildings. Today, Venezuela is famous for combining traditional building elements with modern abstract ones. The Venezuelan capital city of Caracas is one of the most modern cities in the world.

21

HISTORICAL INSPIRATION

History and people are the main inspiration for Venezuelan writers. Before Venezuela gained independence from Spain, many of the books in the country were about the government. This included writings from Simón Bolívar, the head of the independence movement. After the country won its independence in the early 1800s, other **genres** became popular again.

The most popular genre in Venezuela is historical fiction. Many writers have written about the Venezuelan War of Independence and the Spanish conquistadors. Conquistadors were Spanish soldiers who explored and conquered parts of the Americas. Venezuela's most famous novel is *Doña Bárbara* (1929) by Rómulo Gallegos. It's about a cruel leader.

Arturo Uslar Pietri was a Venezuelan novelist, journalist, and politician. He was one of the first Latin American writers to use magical realism, a style that adds unreal, or imaginary, features to everyday occurrences.

Andrés Bello was a poet who is considered to be the father of Latin American intellectualism. Intellectualism is the belief that reason is more important than emotions.

The Legend of *El Dorado*

El Dorado (the golden one) is a legendary native ruler who, stories say, covered himself in gold dust during festivals and then jumped into a lake to wash it off. This story and the discovery of gold along the coast of Latin America inspired many to believe there was a beautiful city of gold located within South America. This drove many Spanish explorers deep into Venezuela and other locations to find the city. No one ever found the city, but the legend has inspired many stories in the area since.

23

POPULAR FOODS

There are three main meals in Venezuela: a large breakfast, a large dinner (around noon), and a light supper. Venezuelans are very friendly and are known to offer lots of food to guests. Beans, rice, fruits, and vegetables are common in Venezuelan dishes, but recipes and ingredients vary across the country. The most famous dishes are arepas (cornmeal bread) and *hallacas* (corn dough stuffed with meat and wrapped in banana leaves). *Hallacas* are traditionally served around Christmas.

Other foods include filled pastries such as *cachapas*. *Tequeños*, a dish named for the city of Los Teques, are pastries filled with cheese or chocolate. During the Carnival season, more complicated dishes are made. Paella and *talcari de chivo*, or stew, are common.

pabellón criollo

This photo shows cacao that has been gathered. Venezuela produces 15,000 tons (13,607 mt) of cacao a year. Cacao beans are popular all over the world.

Special Dishes

The national dish of Venezuela, *pabellón criollo*, is made with rice, black beans, and shredded beef. It may also contain plantains, peppers, or a fried egg. Many believe this dish is a symbol of the many cultures that have shaped Venezuela, with the brown meat standing for indigenous people, white rice standing for the Europeans, and black beans for the African people brought to the country. Others see each food item as a symbol for the blending of Venezuelan cultures.

25

GAMES AND SPORTS

Baseball is the official sport of Venezuela. Eight teams play in Venezuela's professional baseball league. Many Venezuelan players have gone on to play for American teams, including the New York Yankees, the Chicago Cubs, and the Cincinnati Reds. Other popular sports include soccer, basketball, and boxing. Soccer has become more popular over the past few years.

Horse races and betting are popular pastimes, and Caracas is home to one of the best racetracks in Latin America. Bullfighting is another popular activity, and most Venezuelan cities have their own plaza de toros (bullring). In Caracas, about a dozen bullfights are held each year. They usually take place around the festival of Carnival, when bullfighters from around the world come to compete.

Miguel Cabrera, pictured here, is a famous Venezuelan baseball player.

27

IMPORTANT PEOPLE

Venezuelans celebrate individuals who fought for the rights of their people. One indigenous hero was Guaicaipuro, a native leader who lived in Los Teques and fought the Spanish for almost 10 years. His actions continue to inspire pride in the Venezuelan people.

One of the most important people in Venezuelan history is Simón Bolívar. Bolívar, also known as *El Libertador* (the liberator), was a military leader who led the fight against Spanish rule over Venezuela. His success in battle led to Venezuelan independence. He's the most important person of the Venezuelan independence movement.

After independence, many leaders worked hard to defend Venezuelan freedoms. Rómulo Betancourt, a revolutionary who opposed unfair laws in Venezuela, became president and worked to improve the country.

Yulimar Rojas competed in the 2016 Summer Olympics. Rojas, a track and field athlete, is Venezuela's first world champion in athletics.

A CHANGING CULTURE

Venezuela has changed a lot since the days before the Spanish conquest and War of Independence. Throughout all of these changes, the Venezuelan people have developed their own unique culture. As the country continues to face new challenges, Venezuelan culture will continue to adapt.

There are about 225,000 Venezuelan-born immigrants now living in the United States. This number has risen greatly over the last decade as political conflicts have caused problems in their home country. Almost half the Venezuelan-born immigrants in the United States live in Florida.

Venezuelan Americans have shared their rich cultural traditions with their new communities and country. Exploring other cultures, such as that of Venezuela, is a great way to understand and appreciate what every unique person adds to the world around us.

GLOSSARY

abstract: Art that doesn't represent reality, but uses shapes, forms, colors, and textures to achieve its effect.

ancestor: Someone in your family who lived long before you.

colonization: The act of establishing colonies in a place.

culture: The beliefs and ways of life of a certain group of people.

genre: A style or type of literature or art.

heritage: The traditions and beliefs that are part of the history of a group or nation.

immigrant: A person who comes to a country to live there.

indigenous: Living naturally in a particular region.

legend: A story coming down from the past that is popularly accepted but cannot be checked.

nativity scene: A set of figures showing the birth of Jesus; called a *nacimiento* in Spanish.

nomadic: Having no fixed home and wandering from place to place.

ritual: A religious ceremony, especially one consisting of a series of actions performed in a certain order.

unique: Special or different from anything else.

INDEX

WEBSITES

Due to the changing nature of Internet links, PowerKids Press has developed an online list of websites related to the subject of this book. This site is updated regularly. Please use this link to access the list: www.powerkidslinks.com/chd/venez